# The Life of
# God in the
# Soul of Man

## Henry Scougal

*Vintage Puritan Series*
GLH PUBLISHING
Louisville, Kentucky

Sourced from *The Life of God in the Soul of Man*.
Nicoles & Noyes: Boston, 1868.

GLH Publishing, LLC

ISBN-13: 978-1-941129-10-4

# Contents

# 1. The Occasion Of This Discourse.

My dear friend, this designation doth give you a title to all endeavors whereby I can serve your interests; and your pious inclinations to do so, happily conspire with my duty, that I shall not need to step out of my road to gratify you—but I may at once perform an office of friendship, and discharge an exercise of my function, since the advancing of virtue and holiness, (which I hope you make your greatest study,) is the peculiar business of my employment. This, therefore, is the most popular instance wherein I can vent my affection, and express my gratitude towards you, and I shall not any longer delay the performance of the promise I made you to this purpose; for though I know you are provided with better helps of this nature than any I can offer you, nor are you like to meet with anything here which you knew not before, yet I am hopeful, that what cometh from one whom you are pleased to honor with your friendship, and which is more particularly designed for your use, will be kindly accepted by you; and God's providence perhaps may so direct my thoughts, that something or other may prove useful to you. Nor shall I doubt your pardon, if, for moulding my discourse into the better frame, I lay a low foundation, beginning with the nature and properties of religion, and all along give such way to my thoughts, in the prosecution of the subject, as may bring me to say many things which were not necessary, did I only consider to whom I am writing.

# 2. Mistakes About Religion.

I cannot speak of religion, but I must lament, that among so many pretenders to it, so few understand what it means: some placing it in the understanding, in orthodox notions and opinions; and all the account they can give of their religion is, that they are of this and the other persuasion, and have joined themselves to one of those many sects whereinto Christendom is most unhappily divided. Others place it in the outward man, in a constant course of external duties, and a model of performances. If they live peaceably with their neighbors, keep a temperate diet, observe the returns of worship, frequenting the church, or their closet, and sometimes extend their hands to the relief of the poor, they think they have sufficiently acquitted themselves. Others again put all religion in the affections, in rapturous hearts, and ecstatic devotion; and all they aim at is, to pray with passion, and think of heaven with pleasure, and to be affected with those kind and melting expressions wherewith they court their Savior, till they persuade themselves they are mightily in love with him, and from thence assume a great confidence of their salvation, which they esteem the chief of Christian graces. Thus are these things which have any resemblance of piety, and at the best are but means of obtaining it, or particular exercises of it, frequently mistaken for the whole of religion: nay, sometimes wickedness and vice pretend to that name. I speak not now of those gross impieties wherewith the Heathens were wont to worship their gods. There are but too many Christians who would consecrate their vices, and follow their corrupt affections, whose ragged humor and sullen pride must pass for Christian severity; whose fierce wrath, and bitter rage against their enemies, must be called holy zeal; whose petulancy towards their superiors, or rebellion against their governors, must have the name of Christian courage and resolution.

## 3. What Religion Is.

But certainly religion is quite another thing, and they who are acquainted with it will entertain far different thoughts, and disdain all those shadows and false imitations of it. They know by experience that true religion is a union of the soul with God, a real participation of the divine nature, the very image of God drawn upon the soul, or, in the apostle's phrase, "It is Christ formed within us." Briefly, I know not how the nature of religion can be more fully expressed, than by calling it *a divine life*: and under these terms I shall discourse of it, showing first, how it is called *a life*; and then, how it is termed *divine*.

## 4. The Permanency And Stability Of Religion.

I choose to express it by the name of *life*, first, because of its permanency and stability. Religion it not a sudden start, or passion of the mind, not though it should rise to the height of a rapture, and seem to transport a man to extraordinary performances. There are few but have convictions of the necessity of doing something for the salvation of their souls, which may push them forward some steps with a great deal of seeming haste; but anon they flag and give over. They were in a hot mood, but now they are cooled; they did shoot forth fresh and high, but are quickly withered, because they had no root in themselves. These sudden fits may be compared to the violent and convulsive motions of bodies newly beheaded, caused by the agitations of the animal spirits, after the soul is departed, which, however violent and impetuous, can be of no long continuance; whereas the motions of holy souls are constant and regular, proceeding from a permanent and lively principle. It is true, this divine life continueth not always in that same strength and vigor, but many times suffers sad decays; and holy men find greater difficulty in resisting temptations, and less alacrity in the performance of their duties. Yet it is not quite extinguished, nor are they abandoned to the power of those corrupt affections, which sway and over-rule the rest of the world.

# 5. The Freedom And Unconstrainedness Of Religion.

Again, religion may be designed by the name of *life*, because it is an inward, free, and self-moving principle: and those who have made progress in it, are not actuated only by external motives, driven merely by threatenings, nor bribed by promises, nor constrained by laws; but are powerfully inclined to that which is good, and delight in the performance of it. The love which a pious man bears to God and goodness, is not so much by virtue of a command enjoining him so to do, as by a new nature instructing and prompting him to it; nor doth he pay his devotions as an unavoidable tribute only to appease the divine justice, or quiet his clamorous conscience; but those religious exercises are the proper emanations of the divine life, the natural employments of the new-born soul. He prays, and gives thanks, and repents, not only because these things are commanded, but rather because he is sensible of his wants, and of the divine goodness, and of the folly and misery of a sinful life. His charity is not forced, nor his alms extorted from him; his love makes him willing to give; and though there were no outward obligation, his heart would devise liberal things. Injustice or intemperance, and all other vices, are as contrary to his temper and constitution, as the basest actions are to the most generous spirit, and impudence and scurrility to those who are naturally modest. So that I may well say with St. John, "Whosoever is born of God, doth not commit sin: for his seed remaineth in him, and he cannot sin, because he is born of God." Though holy and religious persons do much eye the law of God, and have a great regard unto it, yet it is not so much the sanction of the law, as its reasonableness, and purity, and goodness, which do prevail with them. They account it excellent and desirable in itself, and that in keeping of it there is great reward; and that divine love wherewith they are actuated, makes them become a law unto themselves:

Quis legem det amantibus?
Major est amor lex ipse sibi.

Who shall prescribe a law to those that love?
Love's a more powerful law which doth them move.

In a word, what our blessed Savior said of himself, is in some measure applicable to his followers, that "it is their meat and drink to do their Father's will." And, as the natural appetite is carried out toward food, though we should not reflect on the necessity of it for the preservation of our lives, so they are carried with a natural and unforced propensity toward that which is good and commendable. It is true, external motives are many times of great use to excite and stir up this inward principle, especially in its infancy and weakness, when it is often so languid that the man himself can scarce discern it, hardly being able to move one step forward but when he is pushed by his hopes or his fears, by the pressure of an affliction, or the sense of a mercy, by the authority of the law, or the persuasion of others. Now, if such a person be conscientious and uniform in his obedience, and earnestly groaning under the sense of his dullness, and is desirous to perform his duties with more spirit and vigor, these are the first motions of the divine life, which, though it be faint and weak, will surely be cherished by the influences of heaven, and grow unto greater maturity. But he who is utterly destitute of this inward principle, and doth not aspire to it, but contents himself with those performances whereunto he is prompted by education or custom, by the fear of hell or carnal notions of heaven, can no more be accounted a religious person, than a puppet can be called a man. This forced and artificial religion is commonly heavy and languid, like the motion of a weight forced upward. It is cold and spiritless, like the uneasy compliance of a wife married against her will, who carries it dutifully toward the husband whom she does not love, out of some sense of virtue or honor. Hence also this religion is scant and niggardly, especially in those duties which do greatest violence to men's carnal inclinations; and those slavish spirits will be sure to do no more than is absolutely required. It is a law that compels them, and they will be loath to go beyond what it stints them to; nay, they will ever be putting such glosses on it, as may leave themselves the greatest liberty. Whereas, the spirit of true religion is frank and liberal—far from such peevish and narrow reckoning; and he who hath given himself entirely unto God, will never think he doth too much for him.

# 6. Religion A Divine Principle.

By this time I hope it doth appear, that religion is with a great deal of reason termed a *life*, or vital principle, and that it is very necessary to distinguish betwixt it and that obedience which is constrained, and depends upon external causes. I come next to give an account why I designed it by the name of Divine Life: and so it may be called, not only in regard of its fountain and original, having God for its author, and being wrought in the souls of men by the power of his Holy Spirit; but also in regard of its nature, religion being a resemblance of the divine perfections, the image of the Almighty shining in the soul of man: nay, it is a real participation of his nature, it is a beam of the eternal light, a drop of that infinite ocean of goodness; and they who are endowed with it may be said to have "God dwelling in their souls, and Christ formed within them."

# 7. What The Natural Life Is.

Before I descend to a more particular consideration of that divine life wherein true religion doth consist, it will perhaps be fit to speak a little of that natural or animal life which prevails in those who are strangers to the other: and by this I understand nothing else, but our inclination and propensity towards those things which are pleasing and acceptable to nature; or self-love issuing forth and spreading itself into as many branches as men have several appetites and inclinations. The root and foundation of the animal life, I reckon to be sense, taking it largely, as it is opposed unto faith, and importeth our perception and sensation of those things that are either grateful or troublesome to us. Now these animal affections, considered in themselves, and as they are implanted in us by nature, are not vicious or blamable; nay, they are instances of the wisdom of the Creator, furnishing his creatures with such appetites as tend to the preservation and welfare of their lives. These are instead of a law unto the brute beasts, whereby they are directed towards the ends for which they were made: but man being made for higher purposes, and to be guided by more excellent laws, becomes guilty and criminal when he is so far transported by the inclinations of this lower life as to violate his duty, or neglect the higher and more noble designs of his creation. Our natural affections are not wholly to be extirpated and destroyed, but only to be moderated and overruled by superior and more excellent principle. In a word, the difference betwixt a religious and wicked man is, that in the one divine life bears sway, in the other the animal life doth prevail.

# 8. The Different Tendencies Of The Natural Life.

But it is strange to observe unto what different courses this natural principle will sometimes carry those who are wholly guided by it, according to
the diverse circumstances that concur with it to determine them; and then,
not considering this doth frequently occasion very dangerous mistakes,
making men think well of themselves by reason of that seeming difference
which is betwixt them and others, whereas, perhaps, their actions do all
the while flow from one and the same original. If we consider the natural
temper and constitution of men's souls, we shall find some to be airy, frol-
icsome, and light, which make their behavior extravagant and ridiculous;
whereas others are naturally serious and severe, and their whole carriage
composed into such gravity as gains them a great deal of reverence and
esteem. Some are of a humorous, rugged, and morose temper, and can
neither be pleased themselves, nor endure that others should be so. But all
are not born with such sour and unhappy dispositions; for some persons
have a certain sweetness and benignity rooted in their natures; and they
find the greatest pleasure in the endearments of society, and the mutual
complacency of friends, and covet nothing more than to have everybody
obliged to them: and it is well that nature hath provided this complexional
tenderness, to supply the defect of true charity in the world, and to incline
men to do something for one another's welfare. Again, in regard to education, some have never been taught to follow any other rules than those
of pleasure or advantage; but others are so inured to observe the strictest
rules of decency and honor, and some instances of virtue, that they are
hardly capable of doing anything which they have been accustomed to
look upon as base and unworthy.

In fine, it is no small difference in the deportment of mere natural men,
that doth arise from the strength or weakness of their wit or judgment,
and from their care and negligence in using them. Intemperance and lust,
injustice and oppression, and all those other impieties which abound in the
world, and render it so miserable, are the issues of self-love, the effect of
the animal life, when it is neither overpowered by religion, nor governed
by natural reason: but if it once take hold of reason, and get judgment and
wit to be of its party, it will many times disdain the grosser sort of vices,
and spring up into fair imitations of virtue and goodness. If a man have
but so much reason as to consider the prejudice which intemperance and
inordinate lust do bring unto his health, his fortune, and his reputation,
self-love may suffice to restrain him; and one may observe the rules of
moral justice, in dealing with others, as the best way to secure his own
interest, and maintain his credit in the world. But this is not all; for this

natural principle, by the help of reason, may take a higher flight, and come nigher the instances of piety and religion: it may incline a man to the diligent study of divine truths; for why should not these, as well as other speculations, be pleasant and grateful to curious and inquisitive minds? It may make men zealous in maintaining and propagating such opinions as they have espoused, and be very desirous that others should submit unto their judgment, and approve the choice of religion which they themselves have made. It may make them delight to hear and compose excellent discourses about the matters of religion; for eloquence is very pleasant, whatever be the subject: nay, some it may dispose to no small height of sensible devotion. The glorious things that are spoken of heaven, may make even a carnal heart in love with it: the metaphors and similitudes made use of in Scripture, of crowns and sceptres, and rivers of pleasure, &c. will easily affect a man's fancy, and make him wish to be there, though he neither understand nor desire those spiritual pleasures which are described and shadowed forth by them: and when such a person comes to believe that Christ has purchased those glorious things for him, he may feel a kind of tenderness and affection towards so great a benefactor, and imagine that he is mightily enamoured with him, and yet all the while continue a stranger to the holy temper and spirit of the blessed Jesus; and what hand the natural constitution may have in the rapturous devotions of some melancholy persons, hath been excellently discovered of late by several learned and judicious pens.

To conclude, there is nothing proper to make a man's life pleasant, or himself eminent and conspicuous in the world, but this natural principle, assisted by wit and reason, may prompt him to it: and though I do not condemn those things in themselves, yet it concerns us nearly to know and consider their nature, both that we may keep within due bounds, and also that we may learn never to value ourselves on the account of such attainments, nor lay the stress of religion upon our natural appetites or performances.

# 9. Wherein The Divine Life Doth Consist.

It is now time to return to the consideration of that *divine life* whereof I was discoursing before; that life which is hid with Christ in God, and therefore hath no glorious show or appearance in the world, and to the natural man will seem a mean and insipid notion. As the animal life consisteth in that narrow and confined love which is terminated on a man's self, and in his propensity towards those things that are pleasing to nature; so the divine life stands in a universal and unbounded affection, and in the mastery over our natural inclinations, that they may never be able to betray us to those things which we know to be blamable. The root of the divine life is faith; the chief branches are love to God, charity to man, purity, and humility: for, as an excellent person hath well observed, however these names be common and vulgar, and make no extraordinary sound, yet do they carry such a mighty sense, that the tongue of man or angel can pronounce nothing more weighty or excellent. Faith hath the same place in the divine life, which sense hath in the natural, being indeed nothing else but a kind of sense, or feeling persuasion of spiritual things; it extends itself unto all divine truths; but in our lapsed estate, it hath a peculiar relation to the declaration of God's mercy and reconcilableness to sinners through a Mediator; and therefore, receiving its denomination from that principal object, is ordinarily termed faith in Jesus Christ.

The *love* of God is a delightful and affectionate sense of the divine perfections, which makes the soul resign and sacrifice itself wholly unto him, desiring above all things to please him, and delighting in nothing so much as in fellowship and communion with him, and being ready to do or suffer any thing for his sake, or at his pleasure. Though this affection may have its first rise from the favors and mercies of God toward ourselves, yet doth it, in its growth and progress, transcend such particular considerations, and ground itself on his infinite goodness, manifested in all the works of creation and providence. A soul thus possessed with divine love, must needs be enlarged, toward all mankind, in a sincere and unbounded affection, because of the relation they have to God, being his creatures, and having something of his image stamped upon them; and this is that charity I named as the second branch of religion, and under which all the parts of justice, all the duties we owe to our neighbor , are eminently comprehended: for he who doth truly love all the world, will be nearly concerned in the interest of every one; and so far from wronging or injuring any person, that he will resent any evil that befalls others, as if it happened to himself.

By *purity*, I understand a due abstractedness from the body, and mastery over the inferior appetites; or such a temper and disposition of mind, as makes a man despise and abstain from all pleasures and delights of sense or fancy, which are sinful in themselves, or tend to extinguish or lessen our relish of more divine and intellectual pleasures; which doth also infer a resoluteness to undergo all those hardships he may meet with in the performance of his duty; so that not only chastity and temperance, but also Christian courage and magnanimity, may come under this head.

*Humility* imports a deep sense of our own meanness, with hearty and affectionate acknowledgment of our owing all that we are to the divine bounty; which is always accompanied with a profound submission to the will of God, and great deadness toward the glory of the world and applause of men.

These are the highest perfections that either men or angels are capable of—the very foundation of heaven laid in the soul; and he who hath attained them, needs not desire to pry into the hidden rolls of God's decrees, or search the volumes of heaven to know what is determined about his everlasting condition; but he may find a copy of God's thoughts concerning him, written in his own breast. His love to God may give him assurance of God's favor to him; and those beginnings of happiness, which he feels in the conformity of the powers of his soul to the nature of God, and compliance with his will, are a sure pledge that his felicity shall be perfected, and continued to all eternity; and it is not without reason that one said, "I had rather see the real impressions of a God-like nature upon my own soul, than have a vision from heaven, or an angel sent to tell me that my name was enrolled in the book of life."

# 10. Religion Better Understood By Action Than By Words.

When we have said all that we can, the secret mysteries of a new nature and divine life can never be sufficiently expressed; language and words cannot reach them: nor can they be truly understood but by those souls that are enkindled within, and awakened unto the sense and relish of spiritual things: "There is a spirit in man; and the inspiration of the Almighty giveth this understanding." The power and life of religion may be better expressed in actions than in words; because actions are more lively things, and do better represent the inward principle whence they proceed; and, therefore, we may take the best measure of those gracious endowments from the deportment of those in whom they reside; especially as they are perfectly exemplified in the holy life of our blessed Savior, a main part of whose business in this world was to teach, by his practice, what he did require of others,—and to make his own conversation an exact resemblance of those unparalleled rules which he prescribed; so that if ever true goodness was visible to mortal eyes, it was then, when his presence did beautify and illustrate this lower world.

# 11. Divine Love Exemplified In Our Savior: His Diligence In Doing God's Will, And His Patience In Bearing It.

That sincere and devout affection wherewith his blessed soul did constantly burn towards his heavenly Father, did express itself in an entire resignation to his will; it was his very "meat to do the will, and finish the work of him that sent him." This was the exercise of his childhood, and the constant employment of his riper age. He spared no travel or pains while he was about his Father's business, but took such infinite content and satisfaction in the performance of it, that when, being faint and weary with his journey, he rested himself on Jacob's well, and entreated water of the Samaritan woman. The success of his conference with her, and the accession that was made to the kingdom of God, filled his mind with such delight, as seemed to have redounded to his very body, refreshing his spirits, and making him forget the thirst whereof he complained before, and refuse the meat which he had sent his disciples to buy. Nor was he less patient and submissive in suffering the will of God, than diligent in the doing of it: he endured the sharpest afflictions and extremest miseries that ever were inflicted on any mortal, without repining thought, or discontented word: for though he was far from a stupid insensibility, or a fantastic or stoical obstinacy, and had as quick a sense of pain as other men, and the deepest apprehension of what he was to suffer in his soul, (as his bloody sweat, and the sore amazement and sorrow which he professed, do abundantly declare,) yet did he entirely submit to that severe disposition of providence, and willingly acquiesced in it.

And he prayed to God, that "if it were possible," (or, as one of the Evangelists hath it, "if he were willing,") "that cup might be removed:" yet he gently added, "nevertheless, not my will, but thine be done." Of what strange importance are the expressions, John xii. 27, where he first acknowledgeth the anguish of his spirit, "Now is my soul troubled," (which would seem to produce a kind of demur,) "and what shall I say?" And then he goes on to deprecate his sufferings, "Father, save me from this hour;" which he had no sooner uttered, but he doth, as it were, on second thoughts, recall it in these words, "But for this cause came I into the world;" and concludes, "Father, glorify thy name." Now, we must not look on this as any levity, or blameable weakness in the blessed Jesus: he knew all along what he was to suffer, and did most resolutely undergo it; but it shows us the inconceivable weight and pressure that he was to bear, which, being so afflicting, and contrary to nature, he could not think of without terror; yet considering the will of God, and the glory which was to redound from him thence, he was not only content, but desirous to suffer it.

## 12. Our Savior's Constant Devotion.

Another instance of his love to God was his *delight in conversing with him by prayer,* which made him frequently retire himself from the world, and, with the greatest devotion and pleasure, spend whole nights in that heavenly exercise, though he had not sins to confess, and but few secular interests to pray for; which, alas! are almost the only things that are wont to drive us to our devotions. Nay, we may say his whole life was a kind of prayer; a constant course of communion with God: if the sacrifice was not always offering, yet was the fire still kept alive; nor was ever the blessed Jesus surprised with that dullness, or tepidity of spirit, which we must many times wrestle with before we can be fit for the exercise of devotion.

## 13. Our Savior's Charity To Men.

In the second place, I should speak of his love and charity toward all men: but he who would express it, must transcribe the history of the gospel, and comment upon it; for scarce any thing is recorded to have been done or spoken by him, which was not designed for the good and advantage of some one or other. All his miraculous works were instances of his goodness as well as his power; and they benefited those on whom they were wrought, as well as they amazed the beholders. His charity was not confined to his kindred or relations; nor was all his kindness swallowed up in the endearment of that peculiar friendship which he carried toward his beloved disciple; but every one was his friend who obeyed his holy commands, John xv. 14. And whosoever did the will of his Father, the same was to him as his brother, sister, and mother.

Never was any unwelcome to him who came with an honest intention, nor did he deny any request which tended to the good of those that asked it: so that what was spoken of that Roman emperor, who, for his goodness, was called the darling of mankind, was really performed by him, that never any departed from him with a heavy countenance, except that rich youth, Mark x., who was sorry to hear that the kingdom of heaven stood at so high a rate, and that he could not save his soul and his money too. And certainly it troubled our Savior, to see that when a price was in his hand to get wisdom, yet he had no heart to it. The ingenuity that appeared in his first address had already procured some kindness for him; for it is said, "and

Jesus, beholding him, loved him:" but must he, for his sake, cut out a new way to heaven, and alter the nature of things, which make it impossible that a covetous man should be happy?

And what shall I speak of his meekness, who could encounter the monstrous ingratitude and dissimulation of that miscreant who betrayed him, in no harsher terms than these, "Judas, betrayest thou the Son of man with a kiss?" What farther evidence could we desire of his fervent and unbounded charity, than that he willingly laid down his life even for his most bitter enemies; and mingling his prayers with his blood, besought the Father that his death might not be laid to their charge, but might become the means of eternal life to those very persons who procured it?

# 14. Our Savior's Purity.

The third branch of the divine life is *purity*, which, as I said consists in a neglect of worldly enjoyment accommodations, in a resolute enduring of all such troubles as we meet with in doing of our duty. Now surely, if ever any person was wholly dead to all the pleasures of the natural life, it was the blessed Jesus, who seldom tasted them when they came in his way; but never stepped out of his road to seek them. Though he allowed others the comforts of wedlock, and honored marriage with his presence, yet he chose the severity of a virgin life, and never knew the nuptial bed: and though at the same time he supplied the want of wine with a miracle, yet he would not work one for the relief of his own hunger in the wilderness; so gracious and divine was the temper of his soul, in allowing to others such lawful gratifications as himself thought good to abstain from, and supplying not only their more extreme and pressing necessities, but also their smaller and less considerable wants. We many times hear of our Savior's sighs, and groans, and tears; but never that he laughed; and but once that he rejoiced in spirit: so that through his whole life, he did exactly answer that character given of him by the prophet of old, that he was "a man of sorrows and acquainted with grief." Nor were the troubles and disaccommodations of his life other than matters of choice; for never did there any appear on the stage of the world with greater advantages to have raised himself to the highest secular felicity. He who would bring together such a prodigious number of fishes into his disciples' net, and, at another time, receive that tribute from a fish which he was to pay to the temple, might easily have made himself the richest person in the world. Nay, without any money, he could have maintained an army powerful enough to have justled Caesar out of his throne, having oftener than once fed several thousands with a few loaves and small fishes; but, to show how small esteem he had of all the enjoyments in the world, he chose to live in so poor and mean a condition, "that though the foxes had holes, and the birds of the air had nests, yet he, who was Lord and heir of all things, had not whereon to lay his head." He did not frequent the courts of princes, nor affect the acquaintance or converse of great ones; but, being reputed the son of a carpenter, he had fishermen, and such other poor people for his companions, and lived at such a rate as suited with the meanness of that condition.

## 15. Our Savior's Humility.

And thus I am brought unawares to speak of his *humility,* the last branch of the divine life; wherein he was a most eminent pattern to us, that we might "learn of him to be meek and lowly in heart." I shall not now speak of that infinite condescension of the eternal Son of God, in taking our nature upon him, but only reflect on our Savior's lowly and humble deportment while he was in the world. He had none of those sins and imperfections which may justly humble the best of men; but he was so entirely swallowed up with a deep sense of the infinite perfections of God, that he appeared as nothing in his own eyes; I mean so far as he was a creature. He considered those eminent perfections which shined in his blessed soul, not as his own, but the gifts of God; and therefore assumed nothing to himself for them, but, with the profoundest humility, renounced all pretences to them. Hence did he refuse that ordinary compellation of "Good Master," when addressed to his human nature, by one who, it seems, was ignorant of his divinity: "Why callest thou me good? there is none good but God only:" As if he had said, 'The goodness of any creature (and such only thou takest me to be) is not worthy to be named or taken notice of. It is God alone who is originally and essentially good.' He never made use of his miraculous power for vanity or ostentation. He would not gratify the curiosity of the Jews with a sign from heaven, some prodigious appearance in the air; nor would he follow the advice of his countrymen and kindred, who would have all his great works performed in the eyes of the world, for gaining him the greater fame. But when his charity had prompted him to the relief of the miserable, his humility made him many times enjoin the concealment of the miracle; and when the glory of God, and the design for which he came into the world, required the publication of them, he ascribed the honor of all to his Father, telling them, "that of himself he was able to do nothing."

I cannot insist on all the instances of humility in his deportment towards men: his withdrawing himself when they would have made him a king; his subjection, not only to his blessed mother, but to her husband, during his younger years; and his submission to all the indignities and affronts which his rude and malicious enemies did put upon him. The history of his holy life, recorded by those who convened with him, is full of such passages as these; and indeed the serious and attentive study of it is the best way to get right measures of humility, and all the other parts of religion which I have been endeavouring to describe.

But now, that I may lessen your trouble of reading a long letter, by making some pauses in it, let me here subjoin a prayer, that might be proper when one, who had formally entertained some false notions of religion, begins to discover what it is.

# 16. A Prayer.

Infinite and eternal Majesty! Author and Fountain of being and blessedness, how little do we poor sinful creatures know of thee, or the way to serve and please thee! We talk of religion, and pretend unto it; but, alas! how few are there that know and consider what it means! How easily do we mistake the affections of our nature, and issues of self-love, for those divine graces which alone can render us acceptable in thy sight! It may justly grieve me to consider, that I should have wandered so long, and contented myself so often with vain shadows and false images of piety and religion; yet I cannot but acknowledge and adore thy goodness, who hast been pleased, in some measure, to open mine eyes, and let me see what it is at which I ought to aim. I rejoice to consider what mighty improvements my nature is capable of, and what a divine temper of spirit doth shine in those whom thou art pleased to choose, and causest to approach unto thee. Blessed be thine infinite mercy, who sentest thine own Son to dwell among men, and instruct them by his example as well as his laws, giving them a perfect pattern of what they ought to be. O that the holy life of the blessed Jesus may be always in my thoughts, and before mine eyes, till I receive a deep sense and impression of those excellent graces that shined so eminently in him! And let me never cease my endeavours, till that new and divine nature prevail in my soul, and Christ be formed within me.

# 17. On The Excellency And Advantage Of Religion.

And now, my dear friend, having discovered the nature of true religion, before I proceed any further, it will not perhaps be unfit to fix our meditations a little on the excellency and advantages of it, that we may be excited to the more vigorous and diligent prosecution of those methods whereby we may attain so great a felicity. But, alas! what words shall we find to express that inward satisfaction, those hidden pleasures, which can never be rightly understood but by those holy souls that feel them? "A stranger intermeddleth not with their joys." Holiness is the right temper, the vigorous and healthful constitution of the soul. Its faculties had formerly been enfeebled and disordered, so that they could not exercise their natural functions; it had wearied itself with endless tossings and rollings, and was never able to find any rest. Now that distemper being removed, it feels itself well; there is due harmony in its faculties, and a sprightly vigor possesseth every part. The understanding can discern what is good, and the will can cleave to it. The affections are not tied to the motions of sense and the influence of external objects, but they are stirred by more divine impressions, are touched by a sense of invisible things.

# 18. The Excellency Of Divine Love.

Let us descend, if you please, into a nearer and more particular view of religion, in those several branches of it which were named before. Let us consider that love and affection wherewith holy souls are united to God, that we may see what excellency and felicity is involved in it. Love is that powerful and prevalent passion, by which all the faculties and inclinations of the soul are determined, and on which both its perfection and happiness depend. The worth and excellency of a soul is to be measured by the object of its love. He who loveth mean and sordid things doth thereby become base and vile, but a noble and well-placed affection doth advance and improve the spirit into a conformity with the perfections which it loves. The images of these do frequently present themselves unto the mind, and, by a secret force and energy, insinuate into the very constitution of the soul, and mould and fashion it unto their own likeness. Hence we may see how easily lovers or friends do slide into the imitation of the persons whom they affect; and how, even before they are aware, they begin to resemble them, not only in the more considerable instances of their deportment, but also in their voice and gesture, and that which we call their mien or air; and certainly we should as well transcribe the virtues and inward beauties of the soul, if they were the object and motive of our love. But now, as all the creatures we converse with have their mixture and alloy, we are always in hazard to be sullied and corrupted by placing our affections on them. Passion doth easily blind our eyes, so that we first approve, and then imitate the things that are blamable in them. The true way to improve and ennoble our souls is, by fixing our love on the divine perfections, that we may have them always before us, and derive an impression of them on ourselves; and, "beholding with open face, as in a glass, the glory of the Lord, we may be changed into the same image, from glory to glory." He who, with a generous and holy ambition, hath raised his eyes towards that uncreated beauty and goodness, and fixed his affection there, is quite of another spirit, of a more excellent and heroic temper, than the rest of the world, and cannot but infinitely disdain all mean and unworthy things; will not entertain any low or base thoughts which might disparage his high and noble pretensions. Love is the greatest and most excellent thing we are masters of and therefore it is folly and baseness to bestow it unworthily. It is indeed the only thing we can call our own: other things may be taken from us by violence, but none can ravish our love. If any thing else be counted ours by giving our love, we give all, so far as we make over our hearts and wills, by which we possess our other enjoyments. It is not possible to refuse him any thing, to whom by love we have given ourselves; nay, since it is the privilege of gifts to receive their value from the mind of the giver, and not to be measured by the event, but by the desire, he who loveth may, in some sense, be said not only to bestow all that he hath, but all things else which may make the beloved person happy; since he doth heartily wish them, and would really give them if they were in his power: in which sense it is that one makes to say, "That divine love doth, in a manner, give God unto himself, by the complacency it takes in the happiness and perfection of his nature." But though this may seem too strained an expression, certainly love is the worthiest present we can offer unto God, and it is extremely debased when we bestow it another way.

When this affection is misplaced, it doth often vent itself in such expressions as point at its genuine and proper object, and insinuate where it ought to be placed. The flattering and blasphemous terms of adoration, wherein men do sometimes express their passion, are the language of that affection which was made and designed for God; as he who is accustomed to speak to some great person, doth perhaps, unawares, accost another with those titles he was wont to give him; but certainly that passion which accounteth its object a deity, ought to be bestowed on him who really is so. Those unlimited submissions, which would debase the soul if directed to any other, will exalt and ennoble it when placed here. Those chains and cords of love are infinitely more glorious than liberty itself; this slavery is more noble than all the empires in the world.

# 19. The Advantages Of Divine Love.

Again, as divine love doth advance and elevate the soul, so it is that alone which can make it happy. The highest and most ravishing pleasures, the most solid and substantial delights that human nature is capable of, are those which arise from the endearments of a well-placed and successful affection. That which embitters love, and makes it ordinarily a very troublesome and hurtful passion, is the placing it on those who have not worth enough to deserve it, or affection and gratitude to requite it, or whose absence may deprive us of the pleasure of their converse, or their miseries occasion our trouble. To all these evils are they exposed, whose chief and supreme affection is placed on creatures like themselves; but the love of God delivers us from them all.

# 20. The Worth Of The Object.

First, I say, love must needs be miserable, and full of trouble and disquietude, when there is not worth and excellency enough in the object to answer the vastness of its capacity. So eager and violent a passion cannot but fret and torment the spirit, when it finds not wherewith to satisfy its cravings; and, indeed, so large and unbounded in its nature, that it must be extremely pinched and straitened, when confined to any creature: nothing below an infinite good can afford it room to stretch itself, and exert its vigor and activity. What is a little skin-deep beauty, or some small degrees of goodness, to match or satisfy a passion which was made for God: designed to embrace an infinite good? No wonder lovers do so hardly suffer any rival, and do not desire that others should approve their passions by imitating it; they know the scantiness and narrowness of the good which they love, that it cannot suffice two, being in effect too little for one. Hence love, "which is as strong as death;" occasioneth "jealousy which is as cruel as the grave," the coals whereof are coals of fire, which hath a most violent flame.

But divine love hath no mixture of this gall. When once the soul is fixed on that supreme and all-sufficient good, it finds so much perfection and goodness, as doth not only answer and satisfy its affection, but master and overpower it too. It finds all its love to be too faint and languid for such a noble object, and is only sorry that it can command no more. It wisheth for the flames of a seraph, and longs for the time when it shall be wholly melted and dissolved into love; and because it can do so little itself, it desires the assistance of the whole creation, that angels and men would conquer with it the admiration and love of those infinite perfections.

# 21. The Certainty To Be Beloved Again.

Again, love is accompanied with trouble, when it misseth a suitable return of affection: love is the most valuable thing we can bestow, and by giving it, we do, in effect, give all that we have; and therefore it must needs be afflicting to find so great a gift despised, that the present which one hath made of his whole heart, cannot prevail to obtain any return. Perfect love is a kind of self-dereliction, a wandering out of ourselves; it is a kind of voluntary death, wherein the lover dies to himself, and all his own interests, nor thinking of them, nor caring for them any more, and minding nothing but how he may please and gratify the party whom he loves. Thus he is quite undone, unless he meets with reciprocal affection; he neglects himself, and the other hath no regard to him: but if he be beloved, he is revived, as it were, and liveth in the soul and care of the person whom he loves; and now he begins to mind his own concernments, not so much because they are his, as because the beloved is pleased to own an interest in them: he becomes dear unto himself, because he is so unto the other.

But why should I enlarge in so known a matter? Nothing can be more clear than that the happiness of love depends on the return it meets with: and herein the divine lover hath unspeakably the advantage, having placed his affection on him whose nature is love, whose goodness is as infinite as his being, whose mercy prevented us when we were his enemies, therefore cannot choose but embrace us when we are become his friends. It is utterly impossible that God should deny his love to a soul wholly devoted to him, and which desires nothing so much as to serve and please him; he cannot disdain his own image, nor the heart in which it is engraven. Love is all the tribute which we can pay him, and it is the sacrifice which he will not despise.

# 22. The Presence Of The Beloved Person.

Another thing which disturbs the pleasure of love, and renders it a miserable and unquiet passion, is absence and separation from those we love. It is not without a sensible affliction that friends do part, though for some little time: it is sad to be deprived of that society which is so delightful; our life becomes tedious, being spent in an impatient expectation of the happy hour wherein we may meet again: but if death has made the separation, as some time or other it must, this occasions a grief scarce to be paralleled by all the misfortunes of human life, and wherein we may pay dear enough for the comforts of our friendship. But O how happy are those who have placed their love on him who can never be absent from them! They need but open their eyes, and they shall every where behold the traces of his presence and glory, and converse with him whom their soul loveth; and this makes the darkest prison, or wildest desert, not only supportable, but delightful to them.

## 23. The Divine Love Makes Us Partake Of An Infinite Happiness.

In fine, a lover is miserable, if the person whom be loveth be so. They who have made an exchange of hearts by love, get thereby an interest in one another's happiness and misery; and this makes love a troublesome passion, when placed on earth. The most fortunate person hath grief enough to mar the tranquillity of his friend; and it is hard to hold out, when we are attacked on all hands, and suffer not only in our own person, but in another's. But if God were the object of our love, we should share in an infinite happiness, without any mixture or possibility of diminution; we should rejoice to behold the glory of God, and receive comfort and pleasure from all the praises wherewith men and angels do extol him. It should delight us, beyond all expression, to consider, that the beloved of our souls is infinitely happy in himself, and that all his enemies cannot shake or unsettle his throne; "that our God is in the heavens, and doth whatever he pleaseth."

Behold, on what sure foundation his happiness is built, whose soul is possessed with divine love, whose will is transformed into the will of God, and whose great desire is, that his Maker should be pleased! O the peace, the rest, the satisfaction that attendeth such a temper of mind!

## 24. He That Loveth God Finds Sweetness In Every Dispensation.

What an infinite pleasure must it needs be, thus, as it were, to lose ourselves in him, and, being swallowed up in the overcoming sense of his goodness, to offer ourselves a living sacrifice, always ascending unto him in flames of love! Never doth a soul know what solid joy and substantial pleasure is, till once, being weary of itself, it renounce all propriety, give itself up unto the Author of its being, and feel itself become a hallowed and devoted thing, and can say, from an inward sense and feeling, "My beloved is mine," (I account all his interest mine own,) "and I am his:" I am content to be any thing for him, and care not for myself, but that I may serve him. A person, moulded into this temper, would find pleasure in all the dispensations of Providence: temporal enjoyments would have another relish, when he should taste the divine goodness in them, and consider them as tokens of love, sent by his dearest Lord and Maker: and chastisements, though they be not joyous, but grievous, would hereby lose their sting, the rod as well as the staff would comfort him: he would snatch a kiss from the hand that was smiting him, and gather sweetness from that severity; nay, he would rejoice, that though God did not the will of such a worthless and foolish creature as himself, yet he did his own will, and accomplished his own designs, which are infinitely more holy and wise.

# 25. The Duties Of Religion Are Delightful To Him.

The exercises of religion, which to others are insipid and tedious, do yield the highest pleasures and delight to souls possessed with divine love. They rejoice when they are called "to go up to the house of the Lord," that they may "see his power and his glory, as they have formerly seen it in the sanctuary." They never think themselves so happy, as when, having retired from the world, and gotten free from the noise and hurry of affairs, and silenced all their clamorous passions (those troublesome guests within,) they have placed themselves in the presence of God, and entertain fellow-ship and communion with him: they delight to adore his perfections, and recount his favors,—and to protest their affection to him, and tell him a thousand times that they love him; to lay their troubles or wants before him, and disburden their hearts in his bosom. Repentance itself is a de-lightful exercise, when it floweth from the principle of love. There is a secret sweetness which accompanieth those tears of remorse, those melt-ings and relentings of a soul returning unto God, and lamenting its former unkindness.

The severities of a holy life, and that constant watch which we are obliged to keep over our hearts and ways, are very troublesome to those who are only ruled and acted by an external law, and have no law in their minds inclining them to the performance of their duty: but where divine love possesseth the soul, it stands as sentinel to keep out everything that may offend the beloved, and doth disdainfully repulse those temptations which assault it: it complieth cheerfully, not only with explicit commands, but with the most secret notices of the beloved's pleasure, and is inge-nious in discovering what will be most grateful and acceptable unto him: it makes mortification and self-denial change their harsh and dreadful names, and become easy, sweet, and delightful things.

But I find this part of my letter swell bigger than I designed, (indeed who would not be tempted to dwell on so pleasant a theme!) I shall endeavour to compensate it by brevity in the other points.

# 26. The Excellency Of Charity.

The next branch of the Divine Life, is a universal charity and love. The excellency of this grace will be easily acknowledged; for what can be more noble and generous than a heart enlarged to embrace the whole world, whose wishes and designs are levelled at the good and welfare of the universe, which considereth every man's interest as its own? He who loveth his neighbor as himself, can never entertain any base or injurious thought, or be wanting in expressions of bounty. He had rather suffer a thousand wrongs, than be guilty of one; and never accounts himself happy, but when some one or other hath been benefited by him: the malice or ingratitude of men is not able to resist his love: he overlooks their injuries, and pities their folly, and overcomes their evil with good; and never designs any other revenge against his most bitter and malicious enemies, than to put all objections he can upon them, whether they will or not. Is it any wonder that such a person be reverenced and admired, and accounted the darling of mankind? This inward goodness and benignity of spirit reflects a certain sweetness and serenity upon the very countenance, and makes it amiable and lovely. It inspireth the soul with a holy resolution and courage, and makes it capable of enterprising and effecting the highest things. Those heroic actions which we are wont to read with admiration, have, for the most part, been the effects of the love of one's country, or of particular friendships: and, certainly, a more extensive and universal affection must be much more powerful and efficacious.

# 27. The Pleasure That Attends Charity.

Again, As charity flows from a noble and excellent temper, so it is accompanied with the greatest satisfaction and pleasure: it delights the soul to feel itself thus enlarged, and to be delivered from those disquieting, as well as deformed passions, malice, hatred, and envy; and become gentle, sweet, benign. Had I my choice of all things that might tend to my present felicity, I would pitch upon this, to have my heart possessed with the greatest kindness and affection towards all men in the world. I am sure this would make me partake in all the happiness of others: their inward endowments and outward prosperity; everything that did benefit and advantage them would afford me comfort and pleasure: and though I should frequently meet with occasions of grief and compassion, yet there is a sweetness in commiseration, which makes it infinitely more desirable than a stupid insensibility: and the consideration of that infinite goodness and wisdom which governs the world, might repress any excessive trouble for particular calamities that happen in it: and the hopes or possibility of men's after happiness, might moderate their sorrow for their present misfortunes. Certainly, next to the love and enjoyment of God, that ardent charity and affection wherewith blessed souls do embrace one another, is justly to be reckoned as the greatest felicity of those regions above; and did it universally prevail in the world, it would anticipate that blessedness, and make us taste of the joys of heaven upon earth.

# 28. The Excellency Of Purity.

That which I named as a third branch of religion, was purity; and you may remember I described it to consist in a contempt of sensual pleasures, and resoluteness to undergo those troubles and pains we may meet with in the performance of our duty. Now, the naming of this may suffice to recommend it as a most noble and excellent quality. There is no slavery so base, as that whereby a man becomes a drudge to his own lusts: nor any victory so glorious, as that which is obtained over them. Never can that person be capable of anything that is noble or worthy, who is sunk in the gross and feculent pleasures of sense, or bewitched with the light and airy gratifications of fancy. But the religious soul is of a more sublime and divine temper; it knows it was made for higher things, and scorns to step aside one foot out of the ways of holiness, for the obtaining any of these.

# 29. The Delight Afforded By Purity.

And this purity is accompanied with a great deal of pleasure. Whatsoever defiles the soul disturbs it too; all impure delights have a sting in them, and leave smart and trouble behind them. Excess and intemperance, and all inordinate lusts, are so much enemies to the health of the body, and the interest of this present life, that a little consideration might oblige any rational man to forbear them on that very score; and if the religious person go higher, and do not only abstain from noxious pleasures, but neglect those that are innocent, this is not to be looked upon as any violent and uneasy restraint, but as the effect of better choice, that their minds are taken up in the pursuit of more sublime and refined delights, so that they cannot be concerned in these. Any person that is engaged in a violent and passionate affection, will easily forget his ordinary gratifications, will be little curious about his diet, or his bodily ease, or the divertisements he was wonted to delight in. No wonder then, if souls overpowered with divine love despise inferior pleasures, and be almost ready to grudge the body its necessary attendance for the common accommodations of life, judging all these impertinent to their main happiness, those higher enjoyments they are pursuing. As for the hardships they may meet with, they rejoice in them, as opportunities to exercise and testify their affection; and since they are able to do so little for God, they are glad of the honor to suffer for him.

# 30. The Excellency Of Humility.

The last branch of religion is humility; and however to vulgar and carnal eyes this may appear an abject, base, and despicable quality, yet really the soul of man is not capable of a higher and more noble endowment. It is a silly ignorance that begets pride. But humility arises from a nearer acquaintance with excellent things, which keeps men from doting on trifles, or admiring themselves because of some petty attainments. Noble and well-educated souls have no such high opinion of riches, beauty, strength, and other such like advantages, as to value themselves for them, or despise those that want them. And as for inward worth and real goodness, the sense they have of the divine perfections, makes them think very meanly of anything they have hitherto attained, and be still endeavouring to surmount themselves, and make nearer approaches to those infinite excellencies which they admire.

I know not what thoughts people may have of humility, but I see almost every person pretending to it, and shunning such expressions and actions as may make them be accounted arrogant and presumptuous, so that those who are most desirous of praise will be loathe to commend themselves. What are those compliments and modes of civility, so frequent in our ordinary converse, but so many protestations of the esteem of others, and the low thoughts we have of ourselves? And must not that humility be a noble and excellent endowment, when the very shadows of it are accounted so necessary a part of good breeding?

# 31. The Pleasure And Sweetness Of An Humble Temper.

Again, this grace is accompanied with a great deal of happiness and tranquility. The proud and arrogant person is a trouble to all that converse with him, but most of all unto himself; everything is enough to vex him; but scarce anything sufficient to content and please him. He is ready to quarrel with anything that falls out; as if he himself were such a considerable person, that God Almighty should do everything to gratify him, and all the creatures of heaven and earth should wait upon him, and obey his will. The leaves of high trees do shake with every blast of wind; and every breath, every evil word will disquiet and torment an arrogant man. But the humble person hath the advantage when he is despised, that none can think more meanly of him than he doth of himself; and therefore he is not troubled at the matter, but can easily bear those reproaches which wound the other to the soul. And withal, as he is less affected with injuries, so indeed he is less obnoxious unto them. "Contention which cometh from pride," betrays a man into a thousand inconveniences, which those of a meek and lowly temper seldom meet with. True and genuine humility begetteth both a veneration and love among all wise and discerning persons, while pride defeateth its own design, and deprives a man of that honor it makes him pretend to.

But as the chief exercises of humility are those which relate unto Almighty God, so these are accompanied with the greatest satisfaction and sweetness. It is impossible to express the great pleasure and delight which religious persons feel in the lowest prostration of their souls before God, when, having a deep sense of the divine majesty and glory, they sink (if I may so speak) to the bottom of their beings, and vanish and disappear in the presence of God, by a serious and affectionate acknowledgment of their own nothingness, and the shortness and imperfections of their attainments; when they understand the full sense and emphasis of the Psalmist's exclamation, "Lord! what is man?" and can utter it with the same affection. Never did any haughty and ambitious person receive the praises and applauses of men with so much pleasure, as the humble and religious do renounce them: "Not unto us, O Lord! not unto us, but unto thy name give glory, for thy mercy, and for thy truth's sake."

Thus I have spoken something of the excellencies and advantages of religion in its several branches; but should be very injurious to the subject, did I pretend to have given any perfect account of it. Let us acquaint ourselves with it, and experience will teach us more than all that ever hath been spoken or written concerning it. But, if we may suppose the soul to be already awakened unto some longing desires after so great a blessedness, it will be good to give them vent, and suffer them to issue forth in some such aspirations as these.

# 32. A Prayer.

Good God! what a mighty felicity is this to which we are called! How graciously hast thou joined our duty and happiness together, and prescribed that for our work, the performance whereof is a great reward! And shall such silly worms be advanced to so great a height? Wilt thou allow us to raise our eyes to thee? Wilt thou admit and accept our affection? Shall we receive the impression of thy divine excellencies, by beholding and admiring them,—and partake of thy infinite blessedness and glory, by loving thee, and rejoicing in thee? O the happiness of those souls that have broken the fetters of self-love, and disentangled their affection from every narrow and particular good! whose understandings are enlightened by thy Holy Spirit, and their wills enlarged to the extent of thine! who love thee above all things, and all mankind for thy sake! I am persuaded, O God, I am persuaded, that I can never be happy, till my carnal and corrupt affections be mortified, and the pride and vanity of my spirit be subdued, and till I come seriously to despise the world, and think nothing of myself. But O when shall it once be? O when wilt thou come unto me, and satisfy my soul with thy likeness, making me holy as thou art holy, even in all manner of conversation? Hast thou given me a prospect of so great a felicity, and wilt thou not bring me unto it? Hast thou excited these desires in my soul, and wilt thou not also satisfy them? O teach me to do thy will, for thou art my God; thy Spirit is good, lead me unto the land of uprightness. Quicken me, O Lord, for thy name's sake, and perfect that which concerneth me: thy mercy, O Lord, endureth for ever, forsake not the works of thine own hands."

# 33. The Despondent Thoughts Of Some Newly Awakened To A Right Sense Of Things.

I have hitherto considered wherein true religion doth consist, and how desirable a thing it is; but when one sees how infinitely distant the common temper and frame of men is from it, he may perhaps be ready to despond, and give over, and think it utterly impossible to be attained. He may sit down in sadness, and bemoan himself, and say, in the anguish and bitterness of his spirit, "They are happy indeed whose souls are awakened unto the divine life, who are thus renewed in the spirit of their minds; but, alas! I am quite of another constitution, and am not able to effect so mighty a change. If outward observances could have done the business, I might have hoped to acquit myself by diligence and care; but since nothing but a new nature can serve the turn, what am I able to do? I could bestow all my goods in oblations to God, or alms to the poor, but cannot command that love and charity, without which this expense would profit me nothing. This gift of God cannot be purchased with money. If a man should give all the substance of his house for love, it would utterly be contemned. I could pine and macerate my body, and undergo many hardships and troubles; but I cannot get all my corruptions starved, nor my affections wholly weaned from earthly things. There are still some worldly desires lurking in my heart, and those vanities that I have shut out of the doors, are always getting in by the windows. I am many times convinced of my own meanness, of the weakness of my body, and the far greater weakness of my soul; but this doth rather beget indignation and discontent, than true humility in my spirit. And though I should come to think meanly of myself, yet I cannot endure that others should think so too. In a word, when I reflect on my highest and most specious attainments, I have reason to suspect, that they are all but the effects of nature, the issues of self-love acting under several disguises; and this principle is so powerful, and so deeply rooted in me, that I can never hope to be delivered from the dominion of it. I may toss and turn as a door on the hinges, but can never get clear off, or be quite unhinged of self, which is still the centre of all my motions; so that all the advantage I can draw from the discovery of religion, is but to see, at a huge distance, that felicity which I am not able to reach; like a man in a shipwreck, who discerns the land, and envies the happiness of those who are there, but thinks it impossible for himself to get ashore."

# 34. The Unreasonableness Of These Fears.

These, I say, or such like desponding thoughts, may arise in the minds of those persons who begin to conceive somewhat more of the nature and excellency of religion than before. They have spied the land, and seen that it is exceeding good, that it floweth with milk and honey; but they find they have the children of Anak to grapple with, many powerful lusts and corruptions to overcome, and they fear they shall never prevail against them. But why should we give way to such discouraging suggestions? Why should we entertain such unreasonable fears, which damp our spirits and weaken our hands, and augment the difficulties of our way? Let us encourage ourselves, my dear friend, let us encourage ourselves with those mighty aids we are to expect in this spiritual warfare; for greater is he that is for us, than all that rise up against us. "The eternal God is our refuge, and underneath are the everlasting arms. Let us be strong in the Lord, and in the power of his might," for he it is that shall "tread down our enemies." God hath a tender regard unto the souls of men, and is infinitely willing to promote their welfare. He hath condescended to our weakness, and declared with an oath, that he hath no pleasure in our destruction. There is no such thing as dispute or envy lodged in the bosom of that ever-blessed Being, whose name and nature is Love. He created us at first in a happy condition; and now, when we are fallen from it, "He hath laid help upon one that is mighty to save," hath committed the care of our souls to no meaner person than the Eternal Son of his love. It is he that is the Captain of our salvation, and what enemies can be too strong for us when we are fighting under his banners? Did not the Son of God come down from the bosom of his Father, and pitch his tabernacle amongst the sons of men, that he might recover and propagate the divine life, and restore the image of God in their souls? All the mighty works which he performed, all the sad afflictions which he sustained, had this for their scope and design; for this did he labour and toil, for this did he bleed and die. "He was with child, he was in pain, and hath he brought forth nothing but wind; hath he wrought no deliverance in the earth? Shall he not see of the travail of his soul?" Certainly it is impossible that this great contrivance of heaven should prove abortive, that such a mighty undertaking should fail and miscarry. It hath already been effectual for the salvation of many thousands, who were once as far from the kingdom of heaven as we can suppose ourselves to be, and our "High Priest continueth for ever, and is able to save them to the uttermost that come unto God by him." He is tender and compassionate, he knoweth our infirmities, and had experience of our temptations. "A bruised reed will he not break, and smoking flax will he not quench, till he send forth judgment unto victory." He hath sent out his Holy Spirit, whose sweet but powerful breathings are still moving up and down in the world, to quicken and revive the souls of men, and awaken them unto the sense and feeling of those divine things for which they were made, and is ready to assist such weak and languishing creatures as we are, in our essays towards holiness and felicity: and when once it hath taken hold of a soul, and kindled in it the smallest spark of divine love, it will be sure to preserve and cherish, and bring it forth into a flame, "which many waters shall not quench, neither shall the floods be able to drown it." Whenever this day begins to dawn, "and the day-star to arise in the heart," it will easily dispel the powers of darkness, and make ignorance and folly, and all the corrupt and selfish affections of men, flee away as fast before it as the shades of night, when the sun cometh out of his chambers: "For the path of the just is as the shining light, which shineth more and more unto the perfect day. They shall go on from strength to strength, till every one of them appear before God in Zion."

Why should we think it impossible, that true goodness and universal love should ever come to sway and prevail in our souls? Is not this their primitive state and condition, their native and genuine constitution, as they came first from the hands of their Maker? Sin and corruption are but usurpers, and though they have long kept possession, "yet from the beginning it was not so." That inordinate self-love, which one would think were rooted in our very being, and interwoven with the constitution of our nature, is nevertheless of a foreign extraction, and had no place at all in the state of integrity. We have still so much reason left as to condemn it; our understandings are easily convinced, that we ought to be wholly devoted to him from whom we have our being, and to love him infinitely more than ourselves, who is infinitely better than we; and our wills would readily comply with this, if they were not disordered and put out of tune: and is not he who made our souls, able to rectify and mend them again? Shall we not be able, by his assistance, to vanquish and expel those violent intruders, "and turn unto flight the armies of the aliens?"

No sooner shall we take up arms in this holy war, but we shall have all the saints on earth, and all the angels in heaven, engaged on our party. The holy church throughout the world is daily interceding with God for the success of all such endeavours; and, doubtless, those heavenly hosts above are nearly concerned in the interests of religion, and infinitely desirous to see the divine life thriving and prevailing in this inferior world; and that the will of God may be done by us on earth, as it is done by themselves in heaven. And may we not then encourage ourselves, as the prophet did His servant, when he showed him the horses and chariots of fire, "Fear not, for they that be with us are more than they that be against us?"

# 35. We Must Do What We Can, And Depend On The Divine Assistance.

Away then with all perplexing fears and desponding thoughts. To undertake vigorously, and rely confidently on the divine assistance, is more than half the conquest. "Let us arise and be doing, and the Lord will be with us." It is true, religion in the souls of men is the immediate work of God, and all our natural endeavours can neither produce it alone, nor merit those supernatural aids by which it must be wrought. The Holy Ghost must come upon us, and the power of the Highest must overthrow us, before that holy thing can be begotten, and Christ be formed in us. But yet we must not expect that this whole work should be done without any concurring endeavours of our own. We must not lie loitering in the ditch, and wait till

Omnipotence pull us from thence. No, no: we must bestir ourselves, and actuate those powers which we have already received. We must put forth ourselves to our utmost capacities, and then we may hope that "our labour shall not be in vain in the Lord." All the art and industry of man cannot form the smallest herb, or make a stalk of corn to grow in the field; it is the energy of nature, and the influences of Heaven, which produce this effect. It is God "who causeth the grass to grow, and herb for the service of man;" and yet nobody will say, that the labours of the husbandman are useless or unnecessary. So, likewise, the human soul is immediately created by God. It is he who both formeth and enliveneth the child; and yet he hath appointed the marriage-bed as the ordinary means for the propagation of mankind. Though there must intervene a stroke of Omnipotence to effect this mighty change in our souls, yet ought we to do what we can to fit and prepare ourselves; for we must break up our fallow ground, and root out the weeds, and pull up the thorns, that so we may be more ready to receive the seeds of grace, and the dew of heaven. It is true, God hath been found of some who sought Him not. He hath cast himself in their way, who were quite out of his. He hath laid hold upon them, and stopped their course on a sudden; for so was St. Paul converted in his journey to Damascus. But certainly this is not God's ordinary method of dealing with men. Though he hath not tied himself to means, yet he hath tied us to the use of them; and we have never more reason to expect the divine assistance, than when we are doing our utmost endeavours. It shall therefore be my next work, to show what course we ought to take for attaining that blessed temper I have hitherto described. But here, if, in delivering my own thoughts, I shall chance to differ from what is or may be said by others in this matter, I would not be thought to contradict and oppose them, more than physicians do, when they prescribe several remedies for the same disease, which perhaps are all useful and good. "Every one may propose the method he judges most proper and convenient; but he doth not thereby pretend that the cure can never be effected, unless that be exactly observed. I doubt it hath occasioned much unnecessary disquietude to some holy persons, that they have not found such a regular and orderly transaction in their souls, as they have seen described in books; that they have not passed through all those steps and stages of conversion, which some (who perhaps have felt them in themselves) have too peremptorily prescribed unto others. God hath several ways of dealing with the souls of men, and it sufficeth if the work be accomplished, whatever the methods have been.

Again, though in proposing directions I must follow that order which the nature of things shall lead to, yet I do not mean that the same method should be so punctually observed in the practice, as if the latter rules were never to be heeded till some considerable time have been spent in practising the former. The directions I intend are mutually conducive one to another, and are all to be performed as occasion shall serve, and we find ourselves enabled to perform them.

## 36. We Must Shun All Manner Of Sin.

But now, that I may detain you no longer, if we desire to have our souls moulded to this holy frame, to become partakers of the divine nature, and have Christ formed in our hearts, we must seriously resolve, and carefully endeavour, to avoid and abandon all vicious and sinful practices. There can be no treaty of peace, till once we lay down these weapons of rebellion wherewith we fight against heaven; nor can we expect to have our distempers cured, if we be daily feeding on poison. Every wilful sin gives a mortal wound to the soul, and puts it at a greater distance from God and goodness; and we can never hope to have our hearts purified from corrupt affections, unless we cleanse our hands from vicious actions. Now, in this case we cannot excuse ourselves by the pretence of impossibility; for sure our outward man is some way in our power. We have some command of our feet, and hands, and tongue, nay, and of our thoughts and fancies too, at least so far as to divert them from impure and sinful objects, and to turn our mind another way; and we find this power and authority much strengthened and advanced, if we were careful to manage and exercise it. In the mean while, I acknowledge our corruptions are so strong, and our temptations so many, that it will require a great deal of steadfastness and resolution, of watchfulness and care, to preserve ourselves, even in this degree of innocence and purity.

## 37. We Must Know What
## Things Are Sinful.

And, first, let us inform ourselves well what those sins are from which we ought to abstain. And here we must not take our measures from the maxims of the world, or the practices of those whom in charity we account good men. Most people have very light apprehensions of these things, and are not sensible of any fault, unless it be gross and flagitious, and scarce reckon any so great as that which they call preciseness: and those who are more serious, do many times allow themselves too great latitude and freedom. Alas! how much pride and vanity, and passion and honor; how much weakness, and folly, and sin, doth every day show itself in their converse and behavior? It may be they are humbled for it, and striving against it, and are daily gaining some ground: but then the progress is so small, and their failings so many, that we have need to choose a more exact pattern. Every one of us must answer for himself, and the practices of others will never warrant and secure us. It is the highest folly to regulate our actions by any other standard than that by which we must be judged. If ever we would cleanse our way, it must be "by taking heed thereto according to the word of God;" and that "word which is quick and powerful, and sharper than any two-edged sword, piercing even to the dividing asunder of soul and spirit, and of the joints and marrow, and is a discerner of the thoughts and intents of the heart," will certainly discover many things to be sinful and hideous, which pass for very innocent in the eyes of the world. Let us therefore imitate the Psalmist, who saith, "Concerning the works of men, by the words of thy lips I have kept myself from the paths of the destroyer." Let us acquaint ourselves with the strict and holy laws of our religion. Let us consider the discourses of our blessed Savior, (especially that divine sermon on the mount,) and the writings of his holy apostles, where an ingenuous and unbiassed mind may clearly discern those limits and bounds by which our actions ought to be confined. And then let us never look upon any sin as light and inconsiderable; but be fully persuaded, that the smallest is infinitely heinous in the sight of God, and prejudicial to the souls of men; and that, if we had the right sense of things, we should be as deeply affected with the least irregularities, as now we are with the highest crimes.

# 38. We Must Resist The Temptations Of Sin, By Considering The Evils They Will Draw On Us.

But now, amongst those things which we discover to be sinful, there will be some unto which, through the disposition of our nature, or long custom, or the endearments of pleasure, we are so much wedded, that it will be like cutting off the right hand, or pulling out the right eye, to abandon them. But must we therefore sit down and wait till all difficulties be over, and every temptation be gone? This were to imitate the fool in the poet, who stood the whole day at the river-side till all the water should run by. We must not indulge our inclinations, as we do little children, till they grow weary of the thing they are unwilling to let go. We must not continue our sinful practices, in hopes that the divine grace will one day overpower our spirits, and make us hate them for their own deformity.

Let us suppose that we are utterly destitute of any supernatural principle, and want that taste by which we should discern and abhor perverse things; yet sure we are capable of some considerations which may be of force to persuade us to this reformation of our lives. If the inward deformity and heinous nature of sin cannot affect us, at least we may be frightened by those dreadful consequences that attend it: that same selfish principle which pusheth us forward unto the pursuit of sinful pleasures, will make us loath to buy them at the rate of everlasting misery. Thus we may encounter self-love with its own weapons, and employ one natural inclination for repressing the exorbitances of another. Let us therefore accustom ourselves to consider seriously, what a fearful thing it must needs be to irritate and offend that infinite Being on whom we hang and depend every moment, who needs but to withdraw his mercies to make us miserable, or his assistance to make us nothing. Let us frequently remember the shortness and uncertainty of our lives, and how that, after we have taken a few more turns in the world, and conversed a little longer amongst men, we must all go down unto the dark and silent grave, and carry nothing along with us but anguish and regret for all our sinful enjoyments; and then think what horror must needs seize the guilty soul, to find itself naked and all alone before the severe and impartial Judge of the world, to render an exact account, not only of its more important and considerable transactions, but of every word that the tongue hath uttered, and the swiftest and most secret thought that ever passed through the mind. Let us sometimes represent unto ourselves the terrors of that dreadful day, when the foundation of the earth shall be shaken, and the heavens shall pass away with a great noise, and the elements shall melt with fervent heat, and the present frame of nature be dissolved, and our eyes shall see the blessed Jesus, (who came once into the world in all humility to visit us, to purchase pardon for us, and beseech us to accept of it,) now appearing in the majesty of his glory, and descending from heaven in a flaming fire, to take vengeance on those that have despised his mercy, and persisted in rebellion against him. When all the hidden things of darkness shall be brought to light, and the counsels of the heart shall be made manifest; when those secret impurities and subtle frauds whereof the world did never suspect us, shall be exposed and laid open to public view, and many thousand actions which we never dreamed to be sinful, or else had altogether forgotten, shall be charged home upon our consciences, with such evident convictions of guilt, that we shall neither be able to deny nor excuse them. Then shall all the angels in heaven, and all the saints that ever lived on the earth, approve that dreadful sentence which shall be passed on wicked men; and those who perhaps did love and esteem them when they lived in the world, shall look upon them with indignation and abhorrence, and never make one request for their deliverance. Let us consider the eternal punishment of damned souls, which are shadowed forth in Scripture by metaphors taken from those things that are most terrible and grievous in the world, and yet all do not suffice to convey into our minds any full apprehensions of them. When we have joined together the importance of all these expressions, and added unto them whatever our fancy can conceive of misery and torment, we must still remember, that all this comes infinitely short of the truth and reality of the thing.

It is true, this is a sad and melancholy subject; there is anguish and horror in the consideration of it; but sure it must be infinitely more dreadful to endure it: and such thoughts as these may be very useful to fright us from the courses that would lead us thither; how fond soever we may be of sinful pleasures, the fear of hell would make us abstain. Our most forward inclinations will startle and give back, when pressed with that question in the prophet, "Who amongst us can dwell with everlasting burnings?"

To this very purpose it is that the terrors of another world are so frequently represented in holy writ, and that in such terms as are most proper to affect and influence a carnal mind: these fears can never suffice to make any person truly good; but certainly they may restrain us from much evil, and have often made way for more ingenious and kindly impressions.

# 39. We Must Keep A Constant Watch Over Ourselves.

But it will not suffice to consider these things once and again, nor to form some resolutions of abandoning our sins, unless we maintain a constant guard, and be continually watching against them. Sometimes the mind is awakened to see the dismal consequences of a vicious life, and straight we are resolved to reform; but, alas! it presently falleth asleep, and we lose that prospect which we had of things, and then temptations take the advantage; they solicit and importune us continually, and so do frequently engage our consent before we are aware. It is the folly and ruin of most people to live at adventure, and take part in every thing that comes in their way, seldom considering what they are about to say or do. If we would have our resolutions take effect, we must take heed unto our ways, and set a watch before the door of our lips, and examine the motions that arise in our hearts, and cause them to tell us whence they come, and whither they go; whether it be pride or passion, or any corrupt and vicious humor, that prompteth us to any design, and whether God will be offended or any body harmed by it. And if we have no time for long reasonings, let us at least turn our eyes toward God, and place ourselves in his presence, to ask his leave and approbation for what we do. Let us consider ourselves under the all-seeing eye of that divine Majesty, as in the midst of an infinite globe of light, which compasseth us about both behind and before, and pierceth to the innermost corners of the soul. The sense and remembrance of the divine presence is the most ready and effectual means, both to discover what is unlawful, and to restrain us from it. There are some things a person could make a shift to palliate or defend, and yet he dares not look Almighty God in the face, and adventure upon them. If we look unto him we shall be lightened; if we "set him always before us, he will guide us by his eye, and instruct us in the way wherein we ought to walk."

# 40. We Must Often Examine Our Actions.

This care and watchfulness over our actions must be seconded by frequent and serious reflections upon them, not only that we may obtain the divine mercy and pardon for our sins, by an humble and sorrowful acknowledgment of them; but also that we may re-enforce and strengthen our resolutions, and learn to decline or resist the temptations by which we have been formerly foiled. It is an advice worthy of a Christian, though it did first drop from a heathen pen, that before we betake ourselves to rest, we renew and examine all the passages of the day, that we may have the comfort of what we have done aright, and may redress what we find to have been done amiss, and make the shipwrecks of one day be as marks to direct our course in another. This may be called the very art of virtuous living, and would contribute wonderfully to advance our reformation, and preserve our innocence. But, withal, we must nor forget to implore the divine assistance, especially against those sins that do most easily beset us: and though it be supposed that our hearts are not yet moulded into that spiritual frame which should render our devotions acceptable; yet, methinks, such considerations as have been proposed to deter us from sin, may also stir us up to some natural seriousness, and make our prayers against it as earnest, at least, as they are wont to be against other calamities: and I doubt not but God, who heareth the cry of the ravens, will have some regard even to such petitions as proceed from those natural passions which himself hath implanted in us. Besides, that those prayers against sin, will be powerful engagements on ourselves to excite us to watchfulness and care; and common ingenuity will make us ashamed to relapse into those faults which we have lately bewailed before God, and against which we have begged his assistance.

# 41. It Is Fit To Restrain Ourselves In Many Lawful Things.

Thus are we to make the first essay for recovering the divine life, by re-
straining the natural inclinations, that they break not out into sinful practices. But now I must add, that Christian prudence will teach us to abstain
from gratifications that are not simply unlawful, and that, not only that
we may secure our innocence, which would be in continual hazard, if we
should strain our liberty to the utmost point; but also, that thereby we may
weaken the force of nature, and teach our appetites to obey. We must do
with ourselves as prudent parents with their children, who cross their wills
in many little indifferent things, to make them manageable and submissive in more considerable instances. He who would mortify the pride and
vanity of his spirit, should stop his ears to the most deserved praises, and
sometimes forbear his just vindication from the censures and aspersions
of others, especially if they reflect only upon his prudence and conduct,
and not on his virtue and innocence. He who would check a revengeful
humor, would do well to deny himself the satisfaction of representing unto
others the injuries which he hath sustained; and if we would so take heed
to our ways, that we sin not with our tongue, we must accustom ourselves
much to solitude and silence, and sometimes with the Psalmist, "hold our
peace even from good," till once we have gotten some command over that
unruly member. Thus, I say, we may bind up our natural inclinations, and
make our appetites more moderate in their cravings, by accustoming them
to frequent refusals; but it is not enough to have them under violence and
restraint.

# 42. We Must Strive To Put Ourselves Out Of Love With The World.

Our next essay must be, to wean our affections from created things, and all
the delights and entertainments of the lower life, which sink and depress
the souls of men, and retard their motions towards God and heaven; and
this we must do by possessing our minds with a deep persuasion of the
vanity and emptiness of worldly enjoyments. This is an ordinary theme,
and every body can make declamations upon it; but, alas! how few understand or believe what they say? These notions float in our brains, and come
sliding off our tongues, but we have no deep impression of them on our
spirits; we feel not the truth which we pretend to believe. We can tell, that
all the glory and splendour, all the pleasures and enjoyments of the world

are vanity and nothing; and yet these nothings take up all our thoughts, and engross all our affections; they stifle the better inclinations of our soul, and inveigle us into many a sin. It may be in a sober mood we give them the slight, and resolve to be no longer deluded with them; but those thoughts seldom outlive the next temptation; the vanities which we have shut out at the doors get in at a postern: there are still some pretensions, some hopes that flatter us; and after we have been frustrated a thousand times, we must be continually repeating the experiment: the least difference of circumstances is enough to delude us, and make us expect that satisfaction in one thing which we have missed in another; but could we once get clearly off, and come to a serious and real contempt of worldly things, this were a very considerable advancement in our way. The soul of man is of a vigorous and active nature, and hath in it a raging and unextinguishable thirst, an immaterial kind of fire, always catching at some object or other, in conjunction wherewith it thinks to be happy; and were it once rent from the world, and all the bewitching enjoyments under the sun, it would quickly search after some higher and more excellent object, to satisfy its ardent and importunate cravings; and, being no longer dazzled with glittering vanities, would fix on that supreme and all-sufficient Good, where it would discover such beauty and sweetness as would charm and overpower all its affections. The love of the world, and the love of God, are like the scales of a balance; as the one falleth, the other doth rise: when our natural inclinations prosper, and the creature is exalted in our soul, religion is faint, and doth languish; but when earthly objects wither away, and lose their beauty, and the soul begins to cool and flag in its prosecution of them, then the seeds of grace take root, and the divine life begins to flourish and prevail. It doth, therefore, nearly concern us, to convince ourselves of the emptiness and vanity of creature-enjoyments, and reason our heart out of love with them: let us seriously consider all that our reason or our faith, our own experience or the observation of others, can suggest to this effect: let as ponder the matter over and over, and fix our thoughts on this truth, till we become really persuaded of it. Amidst all our pursuits and designs, let us stop and ask ourselves, For what end is all this? At what do I aim? Can the gross and muddy pleasures of sense, or a heap of white and yellow earth, or the esteem and affection of silly creatures like myself, satisfy a rational and immortal soul? Have I not tried these things already? Will they have a higher relish, and yield me more contentment tomorrow than yesterday, or the next year than they did the last? There may be some little difference betwixt that which I am now pursuing, and that which I enjoyed before; but sure, my former enjoyments did show as pleasant and promise as fair, before I attained them; like the rainbow, they looked very glorious at a distance, but when I approached I found nothing but emptiness and vapour. O what a poor thing would the life of man be, if it were capable of no higher enjoyments!

I cannot insist on this subject; and there is the less need when I remember to whom I am writing. Yes, my dear friend, you have had as great experience of the emptiness and vanity of human things, and have, at present, as few worldly engagements as any that I know. I have sometimes reflected on those passages of your life wherewith you have been pleased to acquaint me; and, methinks, through all, I can discern a design of the divine Providence to wean your affections from every thing here below. The trials you have had of those things which the world dotes upon, have taught you to despise them; and you have found by experience, that neither the endowments of nature, nor the advantages of fortune, are sufficient for happiness; that every rose hath its thorn, and there may be a worm at the foot of the fairest gourd; some secret and undiscerned grief, which may make a person deserve the pity of those who, perhaps, do admire or envy their supposed felicity. If any earthly comforts have got too much of your heart, I think they have been your relations and friends; and the dearest of these are removed out of the world, so that you must raise your mind towards heaven when you would think upon them. Thus, God hath provided that your heart may be loosed from the world, and that he may not have any rival in your affection, which I have always observed to be so large and unbounded, so noble and disinterested, that no inferior object can answer or deserve it.

# 43. We Must Do Those Outward Actions That Are Commanded.

When we have got our corruptions restrained, and our natural appetites and inclinations towards worldly things in some measure subdued, we must proceed to take such exercises as have a more immediate tendency to excite and awaken the divine life; and, first, let us endeavour conscientiously to perform those duties which religion doth require, and whereunto it would incline us, if it did prevail in our souls. If we cannot get our inward disposition presently charged, let us study at least to regulate our outward deportment: if our hearts be not yet inflamed with divine love, let us, however, own our allegiance to that infinite Majesty, by attending his service and listening to his word, by speaking reverently of his name and praising his goodness, and exhorting others to serve and obey him. If we want that charity, and those bowels of compassion which we ought to have towards our neighbors, yet must we not omit any occasion of doing them good: if our hearts be haughty and proud, we must, nevertheless study a modest and humble deportment. These external performances are of little value in themselves, yet they may help us forward to better things. The apostle indeed telleth us, "that bodily exercise profiteth little;" but he seems not to affirm that it is altogether useless; it is always good to be doing what we can, for then God is wont to pity our weakness, and assist our feeble endeavours; and when true charity and humility, and other graces of the divine Spirit, come to take root in our souls, they will exert themselves more freely, and with less difficulty, if we have before been accustomed to express them in our outward conversations. Nor need we fear the imputation of hypocrisy; though our actions do thus somewhat outrun our affections, seeing they do still proceed from a sense of our duty; and our design is not to appear better than we are, but that we may really become so.

# 44. We Must Endeavor To Form Internal Acts Of Devotion, Charity, &c.

But as inward acts have a more immediate influence on the soul, to mould it to a right temper and frame, so ought we to be most frequent and sedulous in the exercise of them. Let us be often lifting up our hearts toward God; and if we do not say that we love him above all things, let us at least acknowledge, that it is our duty, and would be our happiness, so to do: let us lament the dishonor done to him by foolish and sinful men, and applaud the praises and adorations that are given him by that blessed and glorious company above: let us resign and yield ourselves up unto him a thousand times, to be governed by his laws, and disposed of at his pleasure; and though our stubborn hearts should start back and refuse, yet let us tell him we are convinced that his will is always just and good; and, therefore, desire him to do with us whatsoever he pleaseth, whether we will or not. And so, for begetting in us a universal charity towards men, we must be frequently putting up wishes for their happiness, and blessing every person that we see; and when we have done any thing for the relief of the miserable, we may second it with earnest desires, that God would take care of them, and deliver them out of all their distresses.

Thus should we exercise ourselves unto godliness, and when we are employing the powers that we have, the Spirit of God is wont to strike in and elevate these acts of our soul beyond the pitch of nature, and give them a divine impression; and, after the frequent reiteration of these, we shall find ourselves more inclined unto them, they flowing with greater freedom and ease.

# 45. Consideration A Great Instrument Of Religion.

I shall mention but two other means for begetting that holy and divine temper of spirit which is the subject of the present discourse. And the first is, a deep and serious consideration of the truths of our religion, and that, both as to the certainty and importance of them.—The assent which is ordinarily given to divine truth is very faint and languid, very weak and ineffectual, flowing only from a blind inclination to follow that religion which is in fashion, or a lazy indifferency and unconcernedness whether things be so or not. Men are unwilling to quarrel with the religion of their country, and since all their neighbors are Christians, they are content to be so too: but they are seldom at the pains to consider the evidences of those truths, or to ponder the importance and tendency of them; and thence it is that they have so little influence on their affections and practice. Those "spiritless and paralytic thoughts," (as one doth rightly term them,) are not able to move the will, and direct the hand. We must, therefore, endeavour to work up our minds to a serious belief and full persuasion of divine truths, unto a sense and feeling of spiritual things: our thoughts must dwell upon them till we be both convinced of them, and deeply affected with them. Let us urge forward our spirits, and make them approach the visible world, and fix our minds upon immaterial things, till we clearly perceive that these are no dreams; nay, that all things are dreams and shadows beside them. When we look about us, and behold the beauty and magnificence of this godly frame, the order and harmony of the whole creation, let our thoughts from thence take their flight towards that omnipotent wisdom and goodness which did at first produce, and doth still establish and uphold the same. When we reflect upon ourselves, let us consider that we are not a mere piece of organized matter, a curious and well-contrived engine; that there is more in us than flesh, and blood, and bones, even a divine spark, capable to know, and love, and enjoy our Maker; and though it be now exceedingly clogged with its dull and lumpish companion, yet ere long it shall be delivered, and can subsist without the body, as well as that can do without the clothes which we throw off at our pleasure. Let us often withdraw our thoughts from this earth, this scene of misery, and folly, and sin, and raise them towards that more vast and glorious world, whose innocent and blessed inhabitants solace themselves eternally in the divine presence, and know no other passions, but an unmixed joy and an unbounded love. And then consider how the blessed Son of God came down to this lower world to live among us, and die for us, that he might bring us to a portion of the same felicity; and think how he hath overcome the sharpness of death, and opened the kingdom of heaven to all believers, and is now set down on the right hand of the Majesty on high, and yet is not the less mindful of us, but receiveth our prayers, and presenteth them unto his Father, and is daily visiting his church with the influences of his Spirit, as the sun reacheth us with his beams.

# 46. To Beget Divine Love, We Must Consider The Excellency Of The Divine Nature.

The serious and frequent consideration of these, and such other divine truths, is the most proper method to beget that lively faith which is the foundation of religion, the spring and root of the divine life. Let me further suggest some particular subjects of meditation for producing the several branches of it. And, first, To inflame our souls with the love of God, let us consider the excellency of his nature, and his love and kindness towards us. It is little we know of the divine perfections; and yet that little may suffice to fill our souls with admiration and love, to ravish our affections, as well as to raise our wonder; for we are not merely creatures of sense, that we should be incapable of any other affection but that which entereth by the eyes. The character of any excellent person whom we have never seen, will many times engage our hearts, and make us hugely concerned in all his interests. And what is it, I pray you, that engages us so much to those with whom we converse? I cannot think that is merely the colour of their face, in their comely proportions, for then we should fall in love with statues, and pictures, and flowers. These outward accomplishments may a little delight the eye, but would never be able to prevail so much on the heart, if they did not represent some vital perfection. We either see or apprehend some greatness of mind, or vigor of spirit, or sweetness of disposition; some sprightliness, or wisdom, or goodness, which charm our spirit and command our love. Now these perfections are not obvious to the sight, the eyes can only discern the signs and effects of them; and if it be the understanding that directs our affection, and vital perfections prevail with it, certainly the excellencies of the divine nature (the traces whereof we cannot but discover in every thing we behold) would not fail to engage our hearts, if we did seriously view and regard them. Shall we not be infinitely more transported with that almighty wisdom and good-ness which fills the universe, and displays itself in all the parts of the creation, which establisheth the frame of nature, and turneth the mighty wheels of Providence, and keepeth the world from disorder and ruin, than with the faint rays of the very same perfections which we meet with in our fellow-creatures? Shall we dote on the sacred pieces of a rude and imperfect picture, and never be affected with the original beauty; This were an unaccountable stupidity and blindness. Whatever we find lovely in a friend, or in a saint, ought not to engross, but to elevate our affections: we should conclude with ourselves, that if there be so much sweetness in a drop, there must be infinitely more in the fountain; if there be so much splendour in a ray, what must the sun be in its glory?

Nor can we pretend the remoteness of the object, as if God were at too great a distance for our converse or our love. "He is not far from every one of us; for in him we live, move, and have our being." We cannot open our eyes, but we must behold some footsteps of his glory; and we cannot turn toward him, but we shall be sure to find his intent upon us, waiting as it were to catch a look, ready to entertain the most intimate fellowship and communion with us. Let us therefore endeavour to raise our minds to the clearest conceptions of the divine nature. Let us consider all that his works do declare, or his word doth discover of him unto us; and let us especially contemplate that visible representation of him which was made in our own nature by his Son, who was the "brightness of his glory, and the express image of his person," and who appeared in the world to discover at once what God is, and what we ought to be. Let us represent him unto our minds as we find him described in the gospel, and there we shall behold the perfections of the divine nature, though covered with the vail of human infirmities; and when we have framed unto ourselves the clearest notion that we can of a Being infinite in power, in wisdom, and goodness, the Author and fountain of all perfections, let us fix the eyes of our souls upon it, that our eyes may affect our heart—and while we are musing the fire will burn.

## 47. We Should Meditate On God's Goodness And Love.

Especially, if we hereunto add the consideration of God's favor and good-will towards us; nothing is more powerful to engage our affection, than to find that we are beloved. Expressions of kindness are always pleasing and acceptable unto us, though the person should be otherwise mean and contemptible; but to have the love of one who is altogether lovely, to know that the glorious Majesty of heaven hath any regard unto us, how must it astonish and delight us, how must it overcome our spirits, and melt our hearts, and put our whole soul into a flame! Now, as the word of God is full of the expressions of his love towards men, so all his works do loudly proclaim it. He gave us our being, and, by preserving us in it, doth renew the donation every moment. He hath placed us in a rich and well-furnished world, and liberally provided for all our necessities. He raineth down blessings from heaven upon us, and causeth the earth to bring forth our provision. He giveth us our food and raiment, and while we are spending the productions of one year, he is preparing for us against another. He sweeteneth our lives with innumerable comforts, and gratifieth every faculty with suitable objects. The eye of his providence is always upon us, and he watcheth for our safety when we are fast asleep, neither minding him nor ourselves. But, lest we should think these testimonies of his kindness less considerable, because they are the easy issues of his omnipotent power, and do not put him to any trouble or pain, he hath taken a more wonderful method to endear himself to us: he hath testified his affection to us by suffering as well as by doing; and because he could not suffer in his own nature he assumed ours. The eternal Son of God did clothe himself with the infirmities of our flesh, and left the company of those innocent and blessed spirits who knew well how to love and adore him, that he might dwell among men, and wrestle with the obstinacy of that rebellious race, to reduce them to their allegiance and felicity, and then to offer himself up as a sacrifice and propitiation for them. I remember one of the poets hath an ingenious fancy to express the passion wherewith he found himself overcome after a long resistance: that the god of love had shot all his golden arrows at him, but could never pierce his heart, till at length he put himself into the bow, and darted himself straight into his breast. Methinks this doth some way adumbrate God's method of dealing with men. He had long contended with a stubborn world, and thrown down many a blessing upon them; and when all his other gifts could not prevail, he at last made a gift of himself, to testify his affection and engage theirs. The account which we have of our Savior's life in the gospel, doth all along present us with the story of his love: all the pains that he took, and the troubles that he endured, were the wonderful effects and uncontrollable evidences of it. But, O that last, that dismal scene! Is it possible to remember it, and question his kindness, or deny him ours? Here, here it is, my dear friend, that we should fix our most serious and solemn thoughts, "that Christ may dwell in our hearts by faith; that we, being rooted and grounded in love, may be able to comprehend with all saints what is the breadth, and length, and depth, and heighth; and to know the love of Christ which passeth knowledge, that we may be filled with all the fulness of God."

We ought also frequently to reflect on those particular tokens of favor and love, which God hath bestowed on ourselves; how long he hath borne with our follies and sins, and waited to be gracious unto us—wrestling, as it were, with the stubbornness of our hearts, and essaying every method to reclaim us. We should keep a register in our minds of all the eminent blessings and deliverances we have met with, some whereof have been so conveyed, that we might clearly perceive they were not the issues of chance, but the gracious effects of the divine favor, and the signal returns of our prayers. Nor ought we to embitter the thoughts of these things with any harsh or unworthy suspicions, as if they were designed on purpose to enhance our guilt, and heighten our eternal damnation. No, no, my friend, God is love, and he hath no pleasure in the ruin of his creatures. If they abuse his goodness, and turn his grace into wantonness, and thereby plunge themselves into the greater depth of guilt and misery, this is the effect of their obstinate wickedness, and not the design of those benefits which he bestows.

If these considerations had once begotten in our hearts a real love and affection towards almighty God, that would easily lead us unto the other branches of religion; and, therefore, I shall need say the less of them.

# 48. To Beget Charity We Must Remember That All Men Are Nearly Related Unto God.

We shall find our hearts enlarged in charity toward men, by considering the relation wherein they stand unto God, and the impresses of his image which are stamped upon them. They are not only his creatures, the workmanship of his hands, but such of whom he taketh special care, and for whom he hath a very dear and tender regard, having laid the designs of their happiness before the foundations of the world, and being willing to live and converse with them in all the ages of eternity. The meanest and most contemptible person whom we behold is the offspring of heaven, one of the children of the Most High; and however unworthy he might behave himself of that relation, so long as God hath not abdicated and disowned him by a final sentence, he will have us to acknowledge him as one of him, and as such to embrace him with a sincere and cordial affection. You know what a great concernment we are wont to have for those that do any ways belong to the person whom we love; how gladly we lay hold on every opportunity to gratify the child or servant of a friend; and sure our love towards God would as naturally spring forth in charity towards men, did we mind the interest that he is pleased to take in them, and consider that every soul is dearer unto him than all the material world; and that he did not account the blood of his Son too great a price for their redemption.

# 49. That They Carry God's Image Upon Them.

Again, as all men stand in a near relation to God, so they have still so much of his image stamped on them as may oblige and excite us to love them. In some, this image is more eminent and conspicuous, and we can discern the lovely traces of wisdom and goodness; and though in others it may be miserably sullied and defaced, yet it is not altogether razed—some lineaments at least do still remain. All men are endowed with rational and immortal souls, with understandings and wills capable of the highest and most exalted things; and if they be at present disordered, and put out of tune by wickedness and folly, this may indeed move our compassion, but ought not, in reason, to extinguish our love. When we see a person of a rugged humor and perverse disposition, full of malice and dissimulation, very foolish and very proud, it is hard to fall in love with an object that presents itself unto us under an idea so little grateful and lovely. But when we shall consider these evil qualities as the diseases and distempers of a soul, which, in itself, is capable of all that wisdom and goodness wherewith the best of saints have ever been adorned, and which may, one day, come to be raised to such heights of perfection as shall render it a fit companion for the holy angels; this will turn our aversion into pity, and make us behold him with such resentments as we should have when we look upon a beautiful body that were mangled with wounds, or disfigured by some loathsome disease; and however we hate the vices, we shall not cease to love the man.

# 50. To Beget Purity, We Should Consider The Dignity Of Our Nature.

In the next place, for purifying our souls, and disentangling our affections from the pleasures and enjoyments of this lower life, let us frequently ponder the excellency and dignity of our nature, and what a shameful and unworthy thing it is for so noble and divine a creature as the soul of man, to be sunk and immersed in brutish and sensual lusts, or amused with airy and fantastical delights, and so to lose the relish of solid and spiritual pleasures; that the best should be fed and pampered, and the man and the Christian be starved in us. Did we but mind who we are, and for what we were made, this would teach us, in a right sense, to reverence and stand in awe of ourselves; it would beget a modesty and shamefacedness, and make us very shy and reserved in the use of the most innocent and allowable pleasures.

# 51. We Should Meditate Often On The Joys Of Heaven.

It will be very effectual to the same purpose, that we frequently raise our minds towards heaven, and represent to our thoughts the joys that are at God's right hand, those pleasures that endure for evermore; "for every man that hath this hope in him purifieth himself, even as he is pure." If our heavenly country be much in our thoughts, it will make us as "strangers and pilgrims, to abstain from fleshly lust, which war against the soul," and keep ourselves unspotted from this world, that we may be fit for the enjoyments and felicities of the other. But then we must see that our notions of heaven be not gross and carnal, that we dream not of a Mahometan paradise, nor rest on those metaphors and similitudes by which these joys are sometimes represented: for this might perhaps have a quite contrary effect; it might entangle us farther in carnal affections, and we should be ready to indulge ourselves in a very liberal foretaste of those pleasures wherein we had placed our everlasting felicity. But when we come once to conceive aright of those pure and spiritual pleasures; when the happiness we propose to ourselves is from the sight, and love, and enjoyment of God, and our minds are filled with the hopes and forethoughts of that blessed estate; O how mean and contemptible will all things here below appear in our eyes! With what disdain shall we reject the gross and muddy pleasures that would deprive us of those celestial enjoyments, or any way unfit and indispose us for them!

# 52. Humility Arises From The Consideration Of Our Failings.

The last branch of religion is humility, and sure we can never want matter of consideration for begetting it. All our wickednesses and imperfections, all our follies and our sins, may help to pull down that fond and overweening conceit which we are apt to entertain of ourselves. That which makes any body esteem us, is their knowledge or apprehension of some little good, and their ignorance of a great deal of evil that may be in us; were they thoroughly acquainted with us, they would quickly change their opinion. The thoughts that pass in our hearts, in the best and most serious day of our life, being exposed unto public view, would render us either hateful or ridiculous. And now, however we conceal our failings from one another, yet sure we are conscious of them ourselves, and some serious reflections upon them would much qualify and allay the vanity of our spirits. Thus holy men have come really to think worse of themselves, than of any other person in the world: not but that they knew that gross and scandalous vices are, in their nature, more heinous than the surprisals of temptations and infirmity; but because they were much more intent on their own miscarriages than on those of their neighbors, and did consider all the aggravations of the one, and every thing that might be supposed to diminish and alleviate the other.

## 53. Thoughts Of God Give Us The Lowest Thoughts Of Ourselves.

But it is well observed by a pious writer, that the deepest and most pure humility doth not so much arise from the consideration of our own faults and defects, as from a calm and quiet contemplation of the divine purity and goodness. Our spots never appear so clearly, as when we place them before this infinite light; and we never seem less in our own eyes, than when we look down upon ourselves from on high. O how little, how nothing, do all these shadows of perfection then appear, for which we are wont to value ourselves! That humility, which cometh from a view of our own sinfulness and misery, is more turbulent and boisterous; but the other layeth us full as low, and wanteth nothing of that anguish and vexation wherewith our souls are apt to boil, when they are the nearest objects of our thoughts.

## 54. Prayer, Another Instrument Of Religion, And The Advantages Of Mental Prayer.

There remains yet another means for begetting a holy and religious disposition in the soul, and that is, fervent and hearty prayer. Holiness is the gift of God—indeed the greatest gift he doth bestow, or we are capable to receive; and he hath promised his Holy Spirit to those who ask it of him. In prayer we make the nearest approaches to God, and lie open to the influences of heaven; then it is that the Sun of Righteousness doth visit us with his directest rays, and dissipateth our darkness, and imprinteth his image on our souls. I cannot now insist on the advantages of this exercise, or the disposition wherewith it ought to be performed; and there is no need I should, there being so many books that treat on this subject. I shall only tell you, that as there is one sort of prayer wherein we make use of the voice, which is necessary in public, and may sometimes have its own advantages in private; and another, wherein though we utter no sound, yet we conceive the expressions, and form the words, as it were, in our minds; so there is a third and more sublime kind of prayer, wherein the soul takes a higher flight, and having collected all its forces by long and serious meditation, it darteth itself (if I may so speak) towards God in sighs and groans, and thoughts too big for expression. As when, after a deep contemplation of the divine perfections appearing in all his works of wonder, it addresseth itself unto him in the profoundest adoration of his majesty and glory: for, when after sad reflections on its vileness and miscarriages, it prostrates itself before him with the greatest confusion and sorrow, not daring to lift up its eyes, or utter one word in his presence; or when, having well considered the beauty of holiness, and the unspeakable felicity of those that are truly good, it panteth after God, and sendeth up such vigorous and ardent desires as no words can sufficiently express, continuing and repeating each of these acts, as long as it finds itself upheld by the force and impulse of the previous meditation.

This mental prayer is of all others the most effectual to purify the soul, and dispose it unto a holy and religious temper, and may be termed the great secret of devotion, and one of the most powerful instruments of the divine life; and, it may be, the apostle hath a peculiar respect unto it, when he saith, that "the Spirit helpeth our infirmities, making intercession for us with groanings that cannot be uttered," or, as the original may bear, "that cannot be worded." Yet I do not so recommend this sort of prayer, as to supersede the use of the other; for we have so many several things to pray for, and every petition of this nature requireth so much time, and so great an attention of spirit, that it were not easy therein to overtake them all: to say nothing, that the deep sighs and heavings of the heart, which are wont to accompany it, are something oppressive to nature, and make it hard to continue long in them. But certainly a few of these inward aspirations will do more than a great many fluent and melting expressions.

# 55. Religion Is To Be Advanced By The Same Means By Which It Is Begun; And The Use Of The Holy Sacrament Toward It.

Thus, my dear friend, I have briefly proposed the method which I judge proper for moulding the soul into a holy frame; and the same means which serve to beget this divine temper, must still be practiced for strengthening and advancing it: and therefore I shall recommend but one more for that purpose, and it is the frequent and conscientious use of that holy sacrament, which is peculiarly appointed to nourish and increase spiritual life, when once it is begun in the soul. All the instruments of religion do meet together in this ordinance; and while we address ourselves unto it, we are put to practice all the rules which were mentioned before. Then it is that we make the severest survey of our actions, and lay the strictest obligations on ourselves; then are our minds raised up to the highest contempt of the world, and every grace doth exercise itself with the greatest activity and vigor; all the subjects of contemplation do there present themselves unto us with the greatest advantage; and then, if ever, doth the soul make its most powerful sallies toward heaven, and assault it with a holy and acceptable force. And certainly the neglect or careless performance of this duty, is one of the chief causes that bedwarfs our religion, and makes us continue of so low a size.

But it is time I should put a close to this letter, which is grown to a far greater bulk than at first intended. If these poor papers can do you the smallest service, I shall think myself very happy in this undertaking; at least I am hopeful you will kindly accept the sincere endeavors of a person who would fain acquit himself of some part of that which he owes you.

# 56. A Prayer.

And now, O most gracious God, Father and Fountain of mercy and goodness, who has blessed us with the knowledge of our happiness, and the way that leadeth unto it! excite in our souls such ardent desires after the one, as may put us forth to the diligent prosecution of the other. Let us neither presume on our own strength, nor distrust thy divine assistance: but while we are doing our utmost endeavours, teach us still to depend on thee for success. Open our eyes, O God, and teach us out of thy law. Bless us with an exact and tender sense of our duty, and a knowledge to discern perverse things. O that our ways were directed to keep thy statutes, then shall we not be ashamed when we have respect unto all thy commandments. Possess our hearts with a generous and holy disdain of all those poor enjoyments which this world holdeth out to allure us, that they may never be able to inveigle our affections, or betray us to any sin: turn away our eyes from beholding vanity, and quicken thou us in thy law. Fill our souls with such a deep sense, and full persuasion of those great truths which thou hast revealed in the gospel, as may influence and regulate our whole conversation; and that the life which we henceforth live in the flesh, we may life through faith in the Son of God. O that the infinite perfections of thy blessed nature, and the astonishing expressions of thy goodness and love, may conquer and overpower our hearts, that they may be constantly rising toward thee in flames of devoutest affection, and enlarging themselves in sincere and cordial love towards all the world for thy sake; and that we may cleanse ourselves from all filthiness of flesh and spirit, perfecting holiness in thy fear, without which we can never hope to behold and enjoy thee. Finally, O God! grant that the consideration of what thou art, and what we ourselves are, may both humble and lay us low before thee, and also stir up in us the strongest and most ardent aspiration towards thee. We desire to resign and give up ourselves to the conduct of thy Holy Spirit; lead us in thy truth, and teach us, for thou art the God of our salvation; guide us with thy counsel, and afterwards receive us unto glory, for the merits and intercession of thy blessed Son our Savior. *Amen*.

Made in the USA
Lexington, KY
04 March 2019